Address:

Unanchor Press
P.O. Box 184
Durham, NC 27701
www.unanchor.com

Ordering Information:

Quantity sales. Special discounts are available on quantity purchases by corporations, associations, and others. For details, contact the publisher at the address above.

Orders by U.S. trade bookstores and wholesalers. Please contact Unanchor at hello@unanchor.com, or visit http://www.unanchor.com.

Printed in the United States of America

Unanchor is a global family for travellers to experience the world with the heart of a local.

UNANCHOR

Tangier

The Hotel Continental, Tangier

One Day in Africa - A Guide to Tangier

By Aidan McMahon

Table of Contents

Introduction

============

Interrailing around Europe but yearn for somewhere completely different to end the trip? Trekking around southern Spain and tired of siestas? Or bored of your week-long beach holiday on the Costa del Sol? Then **Tangier**, the gateway to Africa, is the destination for you.

Tangier is surely one of Morocco's most enigmatic cities - an exhilarating, endlessly-fascinating little city undergoing enormous changes.With the strait separating Morocco and Spain a mere 14 km, and the ferry between the two taking just 35 minutes, Tangier is the ideal place to experience North Africa for the first time.

So get your hands on this One-Day Tangier itinerary and prepare yourself for a glimpse into a fascinating culture, country, and continent.

What's inside this Tangier travel guide?

This itinerary will guide you through the city in an accessible and engaging way, from boarding the ferry in Spain right through to your trip back in the evening.

You will see all of the Tangier's main attractions, gain a thorough insight into its history, veer off the beaten path to some intriguing cafés and museums, and take an excursion to the point where the Atlantic and the Mediterranean meet.

The itinerary provides crucial advice on how to avoid scams, shop happily, and eat well, all within a comfortable, flexible schedule that will allow you to enjoy the city's charms.

With detailed maps, local tips, and vivid photos, this guide will set you on course to one of the world's most captivating cities.

Most importantly, most of the attractions are free!

What highlights are included?

- The *medina* (the old part of the city) in all its glory, with a meandering walk from the Sultan's old palace down through crumbling alleys, souks, and courtyards to the main square.
- Mansions, theatres, villas, and consulates which all played host to the city's utterly convoluted recent history (the inspiration for *Casablanca*), and now offer the visitor an enchanting maze of streets to explore.
- Legendary buildings, bookshops, and cafés synonymous with the Beatnik cultural movement and an opportunity to experience the city's unrivalled literary tradition.
- Recommendations for places to eat, how to bargain in the bazaars, and how to make the most of your short stay in Africa.

And much, much more:

- The Hotel Continental and its dazzling mosaics
- The Petit Socco and its animated cafés
- The Cinema Rif, the city's cultural centre
- Two charity groups, to help you get a balanced view of the city
- An obscure art gallery
- An oddly-shaped cave
- Lots of books
- And an obligatory tea, served with mint leaves and as much sugar as you want!

If you decide to stay for longer, there's also advice on hotels, websites, and booklists for further reading.

So what are you waiting for? Grab this indispensable guide and travel with the knowledge that only local experts can provide.

Day 1

=============

9:00 am -- Tarifa to Tangier by Fast Ferry

- **Price:** MAD 850.00 (for a single adult)
- **Duration:** -1 hour and 50 minutes

Catch the **FRS Fast Ferry** from Tarifa in Spain to Tangier, across the Strait of Gibraltar in Morocco.

If you are coming from Gibraltar then it may be easier to buy your tickets in Algeciras, located across the bay from Gibraltar. A bus departs for Tarifa from the port building in Algeciras, and drops you at the departure point for the ferry.

The first ferry departs at 09:00 from the port in Tarifa, and, given the change in timezone between Spain and Morocco, means that you will arrive before 09:00 in the morning in Tangier city port. The cost of a return ticket is approximately $100, or around €75, per person. Ask for your return ticket to be issued also as you expect to return in the evening.

With your tickets you will be given two different coloured immigration and customs forms to fill out. This is a straightforward document. To speed up the process, approach the customs officer on the ferry who will be sitting at a table with a queue of people lining up in front of him. He will look at your passport and the form and give you an entry stamp for Morocco.

When you arrive at the port all you have to do is show your passport with the stamped page, your photograph page, and walk out of the building into Africa.

8:00 am -- The Hotel Continental, the Petit Socco and the Lower Medina

- **Price:** MAD 20.00 (for a single adult)
- **Duration:** 1 hour and 30 minutes
- **Address:** Tangier Medina, Bab Dar Dbagh to Bab Fendaq Zraa

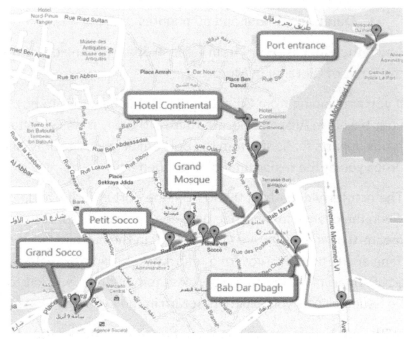

Located directly opposite the town port, the medina is the ideal starting point for exploring Tangier. By immediately immersing yourself in this warren of alleys and lanes you will experience a stimulating introduction to the city.

Local's tip: Use this early morning foray into the medina to appreciate its historic charm without being pestered by shopkeepers and tour guides.

As you exit the port, take a left and continue until you have left the port complex completely. Take in the splendid colonial facades of the seafront buildings and take a right up the busy ramp to **Bab(gate) Dar Dbagh**. You are now entering the medina proper.

Continue on up the lane as it winds its way north along the edge of the medina. You may not see signs for the Hotel Continental, but continue nonetheless.

As you walk, keep an eye out on the right for a very kitsch advertisement for "Jimmy's World Famous Perfumerie - Patronised By Film Stars And The International Jet Set"!

You will soon be at the gate to the hotel. On your left is the **Cafe Des Navegantes**, with its inspired graffiti decoration. This cafe was a haunt of one of Tangier's most celebrated authors, Mohammed Choukri.

Enter and take this opportunity to have your first of many mint teas, or else wait for the selection of cafés in the old town square just after.

The **Hotel Continental** has hosted many well-known foreign visitors since its establishment soon after the formal takeover of Morocco by European powers in 1912.

From the terrace you can enjoy a full view of the city's seafront, extending right around to the other side of the bay, Cape Malabata.

Make sure to enter the hotel, where you can get lost for as long as you like in its lounges, sitting rooms, and libraries. The dining room, inside the building and just above the terrace is also a must see, with a breathtakingly detailed tiled design covering its walls.

Make sure too to grab a free map of the town from the reception!

After walking back down the lane you just came up, take a right when you come to the medina's **Grand Mosque**. The mosque has some impressive features on its outside, but unfortunately you cannot enter if you are a non-Muslim. Continue down this path, the Rue de la Marine, until you reach the Petit Socco.

The **Petit Socco** ("small market"), is the centre of the medina. This early in the morning you will be able to appreciate without interruption the worn charm of the buildings which surround the square.

If you didn't have a tea or a snack in the Hotel Continental, then try the cafe of the **Pension Fuentes** with its pleasant balcony overlooking the square.

This square was the centre of the city, and a natural gathering point for traders, tourists, touts, and other assorted townsfolk. The majority of the buildings on the square are pensions (cheap hotels), cafes, or small shops. Before the expansion of the Ville Nouvelle (everything outside the medina and the old city walls), this was the focal point of Tangier.

Many of the buildings served as post-offices for the occupying European powers, and the facade of the former Spanish post-office can still be made out. This building is now a charitable organisation run by Spanish Franciscan monks who will happily show you around. Just call to the first door on the left on Rue Mokhtar Ahardan. A remnant of a time when Spain a strong grip on Tangier, the organization is now dedicated to helping teenagers and children with disabilities.

In contrast to this establishment is a thoroughly modern French/Moroccan enterprise on the other side of the square and a short way down the busy Rue des Almohades. It is an art gallery which showcases new and exciting pieces by local artists. If it isn't open when you arrive, you will have another opportunity to drop in later.

Continue your tour by walking up the Rue Siaghine. This was one of the most important commercial zones of the city, and still retains a lively commercial atmosphere.

Local's tip: Don't go shopping now, you'll have better opportunities later if you want a souvenir.

At the top of the street is the busy **Bab Fendaq Zraa**. This is the main entrance to the medina, but you'll be exiting here onto the Place 9 Avril, formerly known as the **Grand Socco**. It is the modern centre of the city, a wide roundabout with an assortment of interesting sites surrounding it. Formerly a market, as the name suggests, it is now crowded and busy with a steady stream of taxis and buses.

9:30 am -- St Andrew's Church

- **Price:** FREE
- **Duration:** 30 minutes
- **Address:** Rue d'Angleterre 50, Socco, Tangier, Morocco

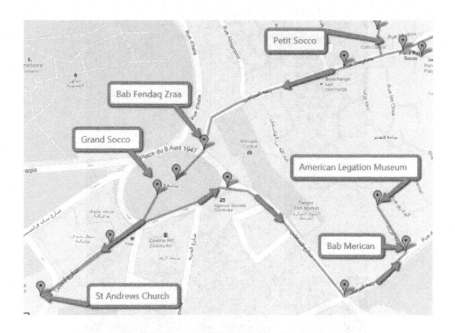

As it is still early, wander across the square and up the Rue
d'Angleterre. Facing you after a short distance is the pleasant
St. Andrews Anglican Church. Open from about 9:30, you can
take some time to wander around its leafy garden and
cemetery. Buried here are the many British and American
(among others) residents of the city from the twentieth century
and before.

Provided the caretaker is around, you can also enter the building. The visit is free, but a donation would be appreciated.

Inside the church is a rare blend of modern Christian and Islamic architecture. Consecrated at the start of the 20th century, the details of its design showcase a unique combination of styles with a heavy Moorish influence.

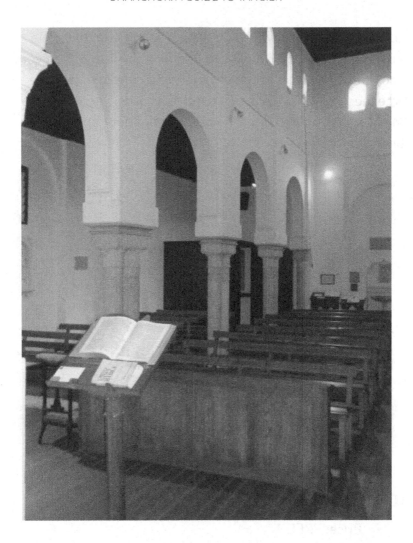

If you are here on a Thursday, the street around the walls will be hectic with the weekly market. Families travel from the foothills of the Rif mountains to sell agricultural produce. Women in multicoloured Rif clothing, including the wide-brimmed hats typical of that region, line the streets surrounded by fresh vegetables and fruit.

Now wander back down to the **Grand Socco** and down the busy market street of Rue Saleh Eddine El Ayoubi. When you reach the busy intersection, turn left and continue with the large medina wall on your left hand side. Soon you will reach **Bab Merican**, named after the next destination on your itinerary.

10:00 am -- The American Legation Museum

- **Price:** FREE
- **Duration:** 45 minutes
- **Address:** 8 Rue d'Amerique, Tangier

Website: www.legation.org

Knock on the door or ring the bell and step into America's first embassy in the world, and one of its only National Heritage Monuments outside of the US. As the first country to recognise US independence, diplomatic ties between the two countries have always been strong. Inside this museum is a wealth of interesting historical material, and the building itself is a pleasure to explore.

Once again, entry is free.

A bizarre letter from the US ambassador explaining how he could not refuse the gift of two lions from the Sultan in the mid-19th century is one highlight. Another feature is part of billionaire tycoon Malcolm Forbes' toy soldier collection, familiar to some visitors from the finale of James Bond classic The Living Daylights.

However, it is the section of the legation that is dedicated to American expatriate writers that steals the show. A remarkable side effect of the internationalisation of Tangier was that it attracted many artists and writers due to its laissez-faire legal and financial regulations. Among these were beatnik writers such as Kerouac, Burroughs, and Brian Gyson. The writer most associated with the city, however, and whose novels and short stories capture masterfully the essence of international Tangier, is Paul Bowles. A dedicated room in the building showcases his letters, photos, books, and recordings.

10:45 am -- Teatro Cervantes

- **Price:** FREE
- **Duration:** 20 minutes
- **Address:** Off the Rue de la Plage, Tangier

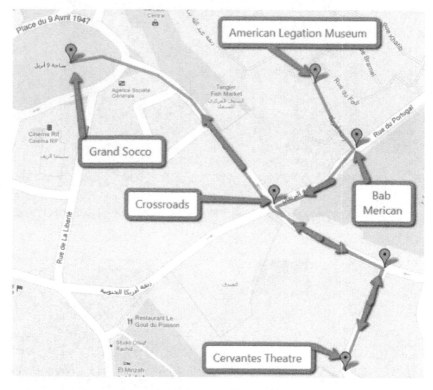

Exit through the **Bab Merican** and take a left down Rue Saleh Eddine El Ayoubi. Passing through the busy street market, continue down until a turn off on the right. Take this and carry on to the end of the street where you can view the magnificent facade of the **Teatro Cervantes**, one of the major architectural contributions by the Spanish to the city.

Return back up the same street to the **Grand Socco** now for something to eat.

11:05 am -- Lunch and the Mendoubia Gardens

- **Price:** MAD 60.00 (for a single adult)
- **Duration:** 1 hour and 15 minutes
- **Address:** Grand Socco/Place 9 Avril, Socco, Tangier

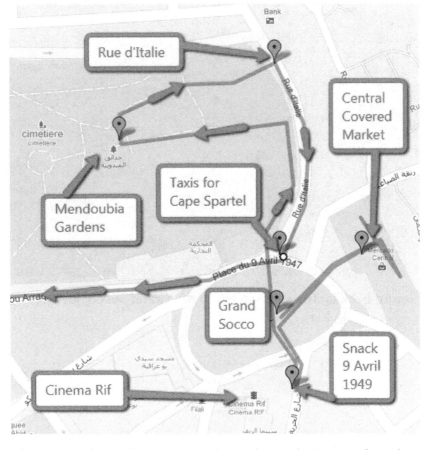

Three or four good options await you here: the **covered market** at the entrance to the medina, where you can buy flat bread, fresh cheese, olives, nuts, fruit, and other delicious food. This option will work out at about $2.

If you want friendly service and some hot sandwiches with a wide range of fillings to choose from, go to **Snack 9 Avril 1949** on the right as you walk up Rue de la Liberté just off the Grand Socco. They make an excellent chicken sandwich but can also make vegetarian snacks. This will cost about $3 with a drink.

Another option on the Grand Socco is the **Cinema Rif**. An excellent venue, the cinema shows a broad selection of Moroccan and international films in a range of languages and with a range of subtitles. It is the alternative centre of the city, with students and artists congregating there in the evenings to discuss the week's films along with everything else. It also does some great snacks, but might push your lunch budget up by a few dollars. A pastry and a coffee will cost about $3.

Finally, DARNA Women's Community Centre and vocational training centre is located just past the cinema Rif and have a delicious fixed menu for lunch (from Monday to Saturday) that costs from $3 to $6. It is a yellow building to your left after you pass the cinema building, on the way to St Andrew's Church.

The association provides shelter and support for women in the city, in addition to street children and other vulnerable groups. Any kind of donation is appreciated and could be a good way to help.

DARNA is an option for your evening meal too, so choose one of the other establishments now if you want to eat there later.

After finishing your snack, it's time to walk north across the Grand Socco to the **Mendoubia Gardens**. Between the end of World War II and 1956, when Morocco gained independence, nationalist groups within the country became increasingly active. Tangier was an important part of this as its special international status allowed nationalist politicians to remain unmolested by the French and Spanish colonial regimes in the rest of the country.

Now a rather shabby park, these gardens were once the site of an historically significant speech by the Sultan of Morocco on 9 April 1947. Expected by the colonial authorities to make the usual pro-regime statements, he outspokenly criticized them instead and made supportive remarks about the nationalist opposition.

The surroundings are pleasant enough, if a little run down.

Directly opposite the park on the Rue d'Italie, which runs along the side of the medina, there are a number of picturesque buildings with baroque details around their windows and balconies.

Return to the **Grand Socco** and flag down an official taxi to arrange your excursion to Cape Spartel.

12:20 pm -- Excursion to Cape Spartel

- **Price:** MAD 250.00 (for a single adult)
- **Duration:** 35 minutes

Before you get in a taxi, try to ascertain whether or not you'll be able to make yourself understood with the driver, who may speak some English and will likely speak French or Spanish. A return trip to **Cape Spartel** and the **Grottes d'Hercule** should cost $20 to $25, waiting time included.

If you find it too difficult to arrange the taxi yourself, call across to the Cinema Rif or Hotel El Minzah (see later in the guide) and ask the staff to call a taxi for you. You will likely find English speakers in both establishments. Above all, don't worry!

Local's tip: *There are a few things to bear in mind when arranging this excursion. Make sure you open the discussion in a friendly way so you and your driver can enjoy the trip. Start by saying "salaam aleykum", meaning "peace be upon you". Enquire then to see if the driver speaks any English (or another language with which you are familiar). Say "Cap Spartel" or simply "Spartel" and "Grottes d'Hercule" clearly and specify that you require that he wait. Crucially, do not pay until you have returned from the trip and are satisfied with the service. See the appendix for information on Moroccan Arabic.*

The drive to the coast is leafy and pleasant, with the road flanked on either side by mansions built by rich expatriates in the early 20th century, and the local Royal Palace can also be spotted on the way.

12:55 pm -- Cape Spartel Lighthouse and the Grottes d'Hercule

- **Price:** MAD 40.00 (for a single adult)
- **Duration:** 1 hour
- **Address:** Cape Spartel, Tangier, Morocco

Approximately twelve kilometres to the west of Tangier is the **Cape Spartel Lighthouse**. Standing discreetly amongst a grove of palm trees, the tower has a squat, unassuming appearance. The neo-Moorish design of its exterior is appealing, however. Looking down to the water from this point, you can plainly see where the Atlantic Ocean meets the Straits of Gibraltar and the Mediterranean Sea, and for this reason this is an enjoyable spot to spend some time. When you've had enough you can continue on to the Grottes d'Hercule.

The **Grottes d'Hercule** are named after Hercules, as the Straits of Gibraltar are said to have been created when he separated the two land masses. All that aside, it's an impressive cave right on the Atlantic coast, and interestingly is shaped like Africa, but in reverse. Appropriate for your day trip to the continent! Entry costs a few *dirham*, roughly $3-4.

1:55 pm -- Taxi back to town

- **Price:** FREE
- **Duration:** 35 minutes

On the way back, ask the driver to drop you off at the **Café Hafa**, just off the Avenue Hadj Mohamed Tazi in the north of the city.

2:30 pm -- The Café Hafa

- **Price:** MAD 20.00 (for a single adult)
- **Duration:** 30 minutes
- **Address:** Ave Hadi Mohammed Tazi, Tangier

The **Café Hafa** is an institution in Tangier. Its unpretentious ambience and tiers of plastic chairs descending casually to the sea make it an exceptionally relaxed place to pass some time. Its main attraction, however, is its unrivalled view of Spain just across the straits. As you sit with the many locals, mainly young people these days, you can contemplate the city's unique location in tranquility.

3:00 pm -- The Kasbah Museum and the Upper Medina

- **Price:** MAD 20.00 (for a single adult)
- **Duration:** 1 hour
- **Address:** North Medina, Tangier

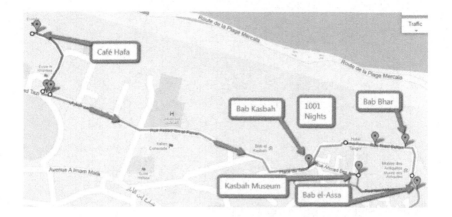

Keep to the left and walk along the Rue Riad Sultan. After a few minutes you will see **1001 Nights** on your right. This was a legendary café and music venue where the Rolling Stones and a number of other inspired visitors spent time.

You will soon see **Bab Bhar** to your left, a small gate in the wall that leads out to the cliff edge of the upper medina. From here you can enjoy a similar view to that of the Café Hafa. This gate was created when an earthquake caused a portion of the wall to collapse.

Continue around to the right and you will come to the square in front of the **Kasbah Museum**, the Place de la Kasbah.

Entry will be approximately $2 for an adult.

The Kasbah Museum holds a fascinating collection of antiquities from prehistoric times up to the 19th century. It offers the opportunity to see objects found at ruins like Volubilis, near Meknes, an important city further south. The main focus is of course on artefacts from the immediate area around Tangier.

However, the most pleasing element of the museum is the building itself. It has served as the palace of the Sultan, has housed European functionaries with power in the city, and has now been refurbished extensively. The highlight is the old garden situated outside the central courtyard in the museum. It is a veritable oasis of serenity compared with the commotion of the rest of the city.

4:00 pm -- Down through the medina

- **Price:** FREE
- **Duration:** 45 minutes
- **Address:** Tangier Medina

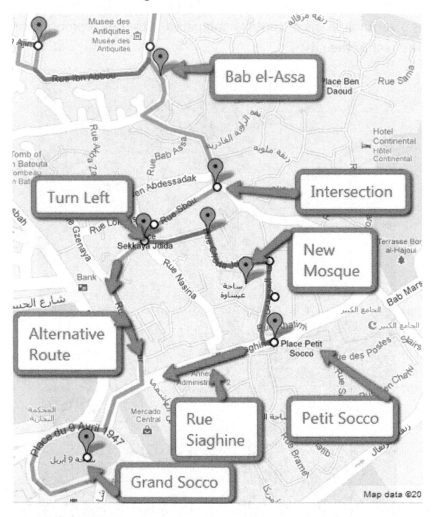

When finished in the museum, you can take another walk back down through the medina, following several small lanes and alleys until you come onto the Rue Des Almohades, or Rue Chorfa Jedid, which will lead you back down to the **Petit Socco**. See the map.

If the art gallery and shop wasn't open when you arrived this morning then now is a good time to pay a visit.

Take this opportunity to look in some of the shops along Rue Siaghine, the street you took earlier to climb up to the **Grand Socco**. If you are not interested in buying anything, continue on to the next section of the itinerary.

Locals tip: *Make sure you bargain. Not only will you be ripped off by paying the original asking price for the product, it's traditionally the way business is done in Morocco. A potentially extended haggling session will accompany most purchases, so be prepared. Try not to rush the process, as it can be enjoyable for both sides if done with good humour. A general rule for getting a reasonable price is to bring the vendor down to half of his first offer. Do this by offering a quarter of what he first says.*

4:45 pm -- Into the Ville Nouvelle: Place de France and the Boulevard Pasteur

- **Price:** MAD 20.00 (for a single adult)
- **Duration:** 45 minutes
- **Address:** Ville Nouvelle, Tangier

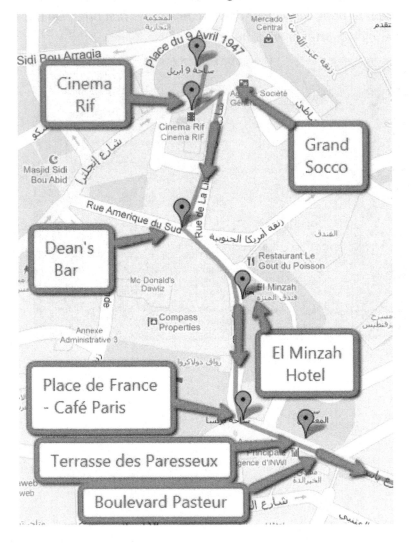

Before you go anywhere, consider returning to DARNA for your evening meal.

From the **Grand Socco**, you can now head south on the Rue de la Liberté and into the heart of the new town, all constructed by the European regimes which controlled the city in the 20th century.

The first relic of mid-20th century Tangier that you will pass is **Dean's Bar**. Dean was one of the city's many larger-than-life characters at the height of the international regime, and he is buried in St Andrew's Church with a headstone that reads "missed by all and sundry". An enigmatic character, his bar was one of the most popular hideaways for the myriad characters based in the city at the time.

The establishment was seemingly the inspiration for Rick's Bar in Casablanca, but nowadays seems to have lost some of its mystique.

Continue up the road. On your left you will see the **Hotel Minzah**. This is one of the city's five star hotels, and served during World War II as the one of the primary meeting points for spies from all over Europe. The city was occupied by the Spanish during the war, and since Spain was technically neutral, the city was one of the few places that opposing diplomats and intelligence operatives would cross paths.

The hotel is still magnificent, although it too has lost some of its old world charm by the construction of a spa and wellness-centre at the back. The central courtyard is, however, truly stunning and **Caid's Bar** and the **Piano Bar** off this central atrium are good choices to stop for a drink, if you have time. Alternatively, the El Korsan restaurant here is an excellent choice for dinner. While more expensive than other options, its consistently excellent service and selection of Moroccan cuisine makes it a great choice.

The best option is to continue on the road to the Place de France where you can stop at the **Café Paris** for an unparalleled sense of the former opulence of the city. This café is a prime people-watching spot too and the many middle-aged men drinking mint tea will be as welcoming as the smartly dressed and courteous staff. The interior's heavy, wooden design and grand chandelier will create a pleasing atmosphere for you to enjoy your tea.

After the Café Paris, turn to the left to make your way down the Boulevard Pasteur. This was the centrepiece of the new city when constructed originally and if you take the time to look up you will see fine examples of art deco styles. On your left is the **Terrasse des Paresseux**, a popular gathering point for locals. It has a charming view of the medina and the Straits. Continue down the boulevard until the end when you can see the **Hotel Rembrandt**.

5:30 pm -- Bookshop, dinner, and back to the port

- **Price:** MAD 100.00 (for a single adult)
- **Duration:** 1 hour
- **Address:** Ville Nouvelle, Tangier

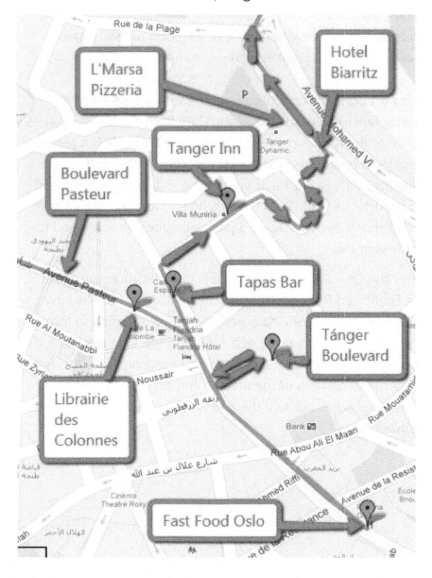

The **Librarie des collonnes** is located on the right side of the Boulevard Pasteur, towards the end where the Hotel Rembrandt is visible.

This bookshop is a Mecca for lovers of literature, especially those interested in Tangier's literary past. There are books in English, French, Spanish, and of course Arabic. The staff are friendly and it is an ideal place to browse and spend some time.

After the bookshop, it's time to get something to eat.

Walk along the Boulevard Mohammed V for several hundred metres until you come to **Oslo Fast Food** on your left. This cheap and cheerful place is usually full of local families feasting on a variety of filling staples. Try the delicious shawarma, better known to some as a kebab. The affable ambience will allow you to experience an authentic meal out with the city's residents, and not the usual artificial tourist set-ups. Expect to pay about $3 to $4 for the meal. To be clear, it is not a formal restaurant.

See later for other options.

When you're finished, you can take a walk back up Mohammed V via Tangier Boulevard, a new complex of flats and shops just off the boulevard and overlooking the beach. It's modern, clean and full of young people chatting and hanging around in groups on the benches. It's a prime example of the kind of investment coming into the city over the past decade. While the benefits for the majority of the population have yet to become clear, this kind of fresh appearance should do something for Tangier's international reputation.

Come back out onto Mohammed V and walk back up to the Hotel Rembrandt. Pass by it on your right and cross the road for a drink and snack. Just before the Casa de Espana restaurant is a great little Spanish tapas bar.

Its name is not printed above the door, but the door itself has glass panels. Inside, copious tapas, or dishes of food to accompany your drink, will be offered and they have a particularly good selection of seafood.

When you are sufficiently satiated, cross the road and turn down the small steps onto Rue Magellan. A rundown and fairly decrepit street, it houses **Hotel El Muniria** and the **Tanger Inn bar**.

This small, family-run hotel and its bar served as the base for the American beatnik literary and cultural movement, and Kerouac, Ginsberg and Burroughs all stayed here. William Burroughs wrote his seminal Naked Lunch in this very hotel. The friendly staff will be happy to let you look around, and to be honest, upstairs doesn't seem to have changed all that much since the 1950s.

Continue down the hill to the seafront where there are two more options for dinner.

To sample more traditional fare there is an extremely pleasant family-run restaurant in the Hotel Biarritz on the seafront. It has couscous, tajine, and bastilla, all highly recommended Moroccan dishes. If you can make it here, have the harira soup as a starter. It is a hearty, flavoursome broth and should be tasted if possible. A meal here will cost about $10.

Otherwise you can call into the L'Marsa Pizzeria, part of the L'Marsa Hotel above. It has filling pasta, spaghetti and pizza, and also has ice-cream for dessert. Expect to pay around $7 to $10.

After this detour it is time to head back to catch the last ferry. See the map for the easiest way to walk back to the port, a walk of only 10 minutes.

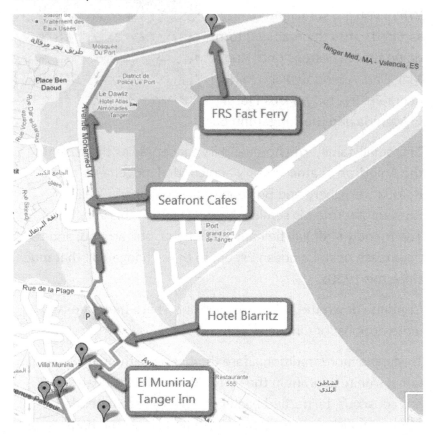

If you find yourself with extra time, any of the small cafés along the seafront where you began your day will offer you a rejuvenating mint tea before the ferry ride at 19:00.

7:00 pm -- Tangier to Tarifa by Fast Ferry

- **Price:** FREE
- **Duration:** 2 hours

As you have already purchased your return ticket, all you have to do is walk back to the port, go through security and board the ferry. If you have any problems find an FRS employee and ask for help. If you happen to miss the ferry, do not fret; the city has a wide range of affordable accommodation and decent hotels are listed in the appendix.

Things You Need to Know (Appendix)

Before you go

If you are taking the ferry from Algeciras or Tarifa to Tangier, it would be a good idea to confirm prices and timetables for the FRS ferry a day in advance. This can be done online, but if you are planning to spend the night before in either of these towns, just call in to one of the many agencies that sell tickets to ask. Depending on the season, you may find that there is an even later ferry back to Spain. This will allow you to linger a bit longer around the city's cafés during your visit. At the same time, ferries can be cancelled due to adverse weather conditions, so try to confirm at the port or by checking the website.

See http://www.frs.es/en/home-area/frs-iberia-ferrys-tarifa-tanger-algeciras-ceuta-tanger-med.html for details.

Transportation tips

If you are planning to use this itinerary then you will realise that the city is actually quite small and can easily be covered on foot. However, taxis are cheap and numerous so make sure to avail of them if you are feeling tired. A short trip across the city in a *petit taxi* (small taxi) should cost approximately $2 to $3, tip included. Arrange this with the driver before you begin or make sure that he has a taximeter. If you are planning to stay longer in the city or in Morocco and plan to use buses to travel onward, you will need to visit the bus station. Its location is shown on the map below. The station can be busy, but be confident and relaxed and simply ignore the touts who will try to help you and then argue about remuneration.

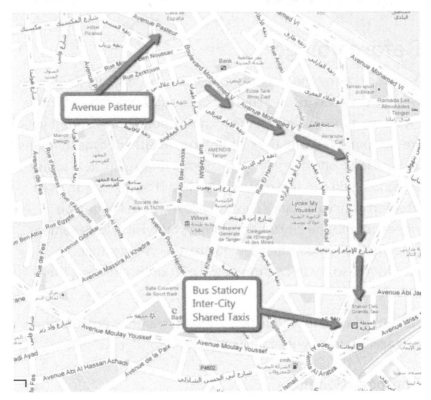

Restaurants

The restaurants and cafés specified in this itinerary are friendly and well-kept establishments. However, there are many cheaper and dirtier places in Tangier. Most of the time you will be fine, but there is a high risk of contracting traveller's diarrhea if you are not careful. Avoid buffets and places which serve a 'special of the week'.

Hotels

If you find yourself stuck in the city then stay at any of the hotels mentioned in the guide. At the cheaper end of the scale, the Hotel Biarritz is a good bet and is located near the port. Expect to pay $10 to $20. The Hotel Continental is also an excellent choice, but costs a bit more due to its interesting past. The Hotel El Muniria is probably the best option at about $25, as it is consistently clean and friendly. For a more romantic option, and an impressive view, the La Tangerina guesthouse is the best choice. It is located near the Kasbah museum. See http://latangerina.com/en/ for more details.

Money

Morocco uses the Moroccan Dirham. You can check the conversion rates between the US Dollar and the Dirham and the Euro and the Dirham here: http://coinmill.com/MAD_USD.html. There is a *bureau de change* on the right before you leave the port area, as well as a number of ATMs. In addition, there are ATMs on the Grand Socco. Make sure you understand the value of the notes before you use them, as the 20dh note can easily be confused with the 200dh note by newly arrived visitors.

Useful local phrases

In Tangier, French, and to a slightly lesser extent Spanish, are widely spoken. Younger Moroccans (especially students), merchants, hotel staff and tourist officials are likely to speak English. The language common to almost all residents of the city is Darija, or Moroccan Arabic. Darija is significantly different to standard Arabic. Some useful phrases and vocabulary can be found at: http://www.linguanaut.com/moroccan.htm

Additional websites and books for information

The following are some interesting websites for more information on the city:

- http://www.tangierdreamer.com/travel_morocco.html
- http://tangerpocket.com/ (French)
- http://www.visitetanger.com/ (French)
- http://www.tangeryotrasutopias.com/ (Spanish)
- http://wikitravel.org/en/Tangier
- http://www.talimblog.org/
- Mohammed Choukri's *For Bread Alone* is a revelatory description of the harsh realities of life on the streets of Tangier, while Tahar Ben Jelloun's *Leaving Tangier* deals with the contemporary issue of illegal migration across the strait to Spain.
- For an indispensable guide to the many fascinating yet challenging visitors that were attracted to the city in the 20th century, Josh Shoemake's 2014 book should be consulted: http://www.amazon.com/Tangier-Literary-Guide-Travellers-Guides/dp/1780762763

Assorted tips

Tangier is safe and should be an extremely enjoyable place to visit. You should, however, be prepared for some hassle from tourist touts and persistent shopkeepers.

When you leave the port, you will likely be approached by someone asking if you need help with anything (hotel, taxi, guide, etc). The best way to deal with this is to firmly but politely say "no" without stopping or engaging with the person. After a while they will give up.

The area outside the port, the medina, and the seafront outside the Hotel Biarritz and Hotel L'Marsa have the highest concentration of hustlers and touts like this. Arriving early in the morning will allow you to avoid the worst of it, but in any case it is not a big problem. Just ignore them and walk confidently. Try not to let it interfere with your visit.

Poverty is a huge problem in Morocco, so you must also be prepared to see extreme contrasts between the rich and the poor. If you want to help, it is a good idea to donate whatever you can to any of the groups mentioned in the guide. Giving money to poor people on the street is an inefficient way to assist, and will reinforce the perception that Westerners are rich and readily dispense money. It may be difficult not to, however, given the sometimes extreme examples of hardship you may come across. If you walk by a beggar without giving some coins, be sure to say "baraka", a blessing which is typically well-received.

About the Author

Aidan McMahon

Originally from Dublin, Ireland, Aidan McMahon is a writer, and lover of languages, history, and cheap hotels.

Unanchor

Chief Itinerary Coordinator

Unanchor wants your opinion.

Your next travel adventure starts now. A simple review on Amazon will grant you and a travel buddy, friend, or human of your choosing any of the wonderful Unanchor digital itineraries for free.

What a deal!

Leave a review

- http://www.amazon.com/unanchor

Collect your guides

- Send an email to reviews@unanchor.com with a link to your review.
- Wait with bated breath.
- Receive your new travel adventure in your inbox!

Other Unanchor Itineraries

Africa

- One Day in Africa - A Guide to Tangier
- Cape Town - What not to miss on a 4-day first-timers' itinerary
- Johannesburg/Pretoria: A 4-Day South Africa Tour Itinerary

Asia

- 4 Days in Bishkek On a Budget
- Beijing Must Sees, Must Dos, Must Eats - 3-Day Tour Itinerary
- 2 Days in Shanghai: A Budget-Conscious Peek at Modern China
- A 3-Day Tryst with 300-Year-Old Kolkata
- Kolkata (Calcutta): 2 Days of Highlights
- 3-Day Budget Delhi Itinerary
- Delhi in 3 Days - A Journey Through Time
- 3 Days Highlights of Mumbai
- Nozawa Onsen's Winter Secrets - A 3-Day Tour
- 3-Day Highlights of Tokyo
- Tour Narita During an Airport Layover
- 3 Days in the Vibrant City of Seoul and the Serene Countryside of Gapyeong
- A First Timer's Weekend Guide to Ulaanbaatar
- The Very Best of Moscow in 3 Days
- Saint Petersburg in Three Days

Central America and the Caribbean

- Old San Juan, Puerto Rico 2-Day Walking Itinerary
- Two Exciting Days in Dutch Sint Maarten - Hello Cruisers!
- Two Amazing Days in St. Croix, USVI - Hello Cruisers!

Europe

- Beginner's Iceland - A four-day self-drive itinerary
- Mostar - A City with Soul in 1 Day
- 3 Days in Brussels - The grand sites via the path less trodden
- Zagreb For Art Lovers: A Three-Day Itinerary
- 3-Day Prague Beer Pilgrimage
- Best of Prague - 3-Day Itinerary
- 3 Days in Copenhagen - Explore Like a Local
- Best of Copenhagen 2-Day Walking Itinerary
- Christmas in Copenhagen - A 2-Day Guide
- 3 Days in Helsinki
- Highlights of Budapest in 3 Days
- 3 Days in Dublin City - City Highlights, While Eating & Drinking Like a Local
- Weekend Break: Tbilisi - Crown Jewel of the Caucasus
- 2 Days In Berlin On A Budget
- A 3-Day Guide to Berlin, Germany
- 3 Days of Fresh Air in Moldova's Countryside
- Amsterdam 3-Day Alternative Tour: Not just the Red Light District
- Amsterdam Made Easy: A 3-Day Guide
- Two-day tour of Utrecht: the smaller, less touristy Amsterdam!
- Krakow: Three-Day Tour of Poland's Cultural Capital
- Best of Warsaw 2-Day Itinerary
- Lisbon in 3 Days: Budget Itinerary
- Braşov - Feel the Pulse of Transylvania in 3 Days
- Lausanne 1-Day Tour Itinerary
- Belgrade: 7 Days of History on Foot

France

- Paris to Chartres Cathedral: 1-Day Tour Itinerary
- A 3-Day Tour of Mont St Michel, Normandy and Brittany
- Art Lovers' Paris: A 2-Day Artistic Tour of the City of Lights
- Paris 1-Day Itinerary - Streets of Montmartre
- Paris 3-Day Walking Tour: See Paris Like a Local
- Paris 4-Day Winter Wonderland
- Paris for Free: 3 Days
- The Best of Paris in One Day

Greece

- Athens 3-Day Highlights Tour Itinerary
- Chania & Sfakia, Greece & Great Day Trips Nearby (5-Day Itinerary)
- Santorini, Greece in 3 Days: Living like a Local

- 2-Day Beach Tour: Travel like a Local in Sithonia Peninsula, Halkidiki, Greece
- Day Trip From Thessaloniki to Kassandra Peninsula, Halkidiki, Greece
- Thessaloniki, Greece - 3-Day Highlights Itinerary

Italy

- A Day on Lake Como, Italy
- 3-Day Florence Walking Tours
- Florence, Italy 3-Day Art & Culture Itinerary
- Milan Unknown - A 3-day tour itinerary
- 3 Days of Roman Adventure: spending time and money efficiently in Rome
- A 3-Day Tour Around Ancient Rome
- Discover Rome's Layers: A 3-Day Walking Tour
- See Siena in a Day
- Landscape, Food, & Trulli: 1 Week in Puglia, the Valle d'Itria, and Matera
- Three Romantic Walks in Venice

Spain

- 3-Day Highlights of Barcelona Itinerary
- FC Barcelona: More than a Club (A 1-Day Experience)
- Ibiza on a Budget - Three-Day Itinerary
- Three days exploring Logroño and La Rioja by public transport
- Málaga, Spain – 2-Day Tour from the Moors to Picasso
- Mijas - One Day Tour of an Andalucían White Village
- Two-Day Tour in Sunny Seville, Spain
- Best of Valencia 2-Day Guide

United Kingdom

- Bath: An Exploring Guide - 2-Day Itinerary
- History, Culture, and Craic: 3 Days in Belfast, Ireland
- 2-Day Brighton Best-of Walks & Activities
- Bristol in 2 Days: A Local's Guide
- Two-Day Self-Guided Walks - Cardiff
- The Best of Edinburgh: A 3-Day Journey from Tourist to Local
- 3-Day London Tour for Olympic Visitors
- An Insider's Guide to the Best of London in 3 Days
- Done London? A 3-day itinerary for off the beaten track North Norfolk
- London 1-Day Literary Highlights
- London for Free :: Three-Day Tour
- London's Historic City Wall Walk (1-2 days)
- London's South Bank - Off the Beaten Track 1-Day Tour
- London's Villages - A 3-day itinerary exploring Hampstead, Marylebone and Notting Hill

- Low-Cost, Luxury London - 3-Day Itinerary
- The 007 James Bond Day Tour of London
- MADchester - A Local's 3-Day Guide To Manchester
- One Day in Margate, UK on a Budget

Middle East

- Paphos 3-Day Itinerary: Live like a local!
- Adventure Around Amman: A 2-Day Itinerary
- Amman 2-Day Cultural Tour
- Doha 2-Day Stopover Cultural Tour
- Doha Surf and Turf: A two-day itinerary
- 3 Days as an Istanbulite: An Istanbul Itinerary
- Between the East and the West, a 3-Day Istanbul Itinerary

North America

Canada

- Relax in Halifax for Two Days Like a Local
- An Insider's Guide to Toronto: Explore the City Less Traveled in Three Days
- The Best of Toronto - 2-Day Itinerary
- Toronto: A Multicultural Retreat (3-day itinerary)

Mexico

- Cancun and Mayan Riviera 5-Day Itinerary (3rd Edition)
- Everything to see or do in Mexico City - 7-Day Itinerary
- Mexico City 3-Day Highlights Itinerary
- Todo lo que hay que ver o hacer en la Ciudad de México - Itinerario de 7 Días
- Your Chiapas Adventure: San Cristobal de las Casas and Palenque, Mexico 5-Day Itinerary

United States

East Coast

- Girls' 3-Day Weekend Summer Getaway in Asheville, NC
- Atlanta 3-Day Highlights
- Baltimore: A Harbor, Parks, History, Seafood & Art - 3-Day Itinerary
- Boston 2-Day Historic Highlights Itinerary
- Navigating Centuries of Boston's Nautical History in One Day
- Rainy Day Boston One-Day Itinerary
- Brooklyn, NY 2-Day Foodie Tour
- The Weekenders Guide To Burlington, Vermont
- A Local's Guide to the Hamptons 3 Day Itinerary
- Weekend Day Trip from New York City: The Wine & Whiskey Trail
- 2 Days Exploring Haunted Key West
- 3 Day PA Dutch Country Highlights (Lancaster County, PA)
- Day Trek Along the Hudson River
- A Local's Guide to Montauk, New York in 2 Days - From the Ocean to the Hills
- New Haven Highlights: Art, Culture & History 3-Day Itinerary
- Day Trip from New York City: Mountains, Falls, & a Funky Town
- 3-Day Amazing Asian Food Tour of New York City!
- Hidden Bars of New York City's East Village & Lower East Side: A 2-Evening Itinerary
- Jewish New York in Two Days
- Lower Key, Lower Cost: Lower Manhattan - 1-Day Itinerary
- New York City - First Timer's 2-Day Walking Tour
- New York City's Lower East Side, 1-Day Tour Itinerary
- New York Like A Native: Five Boroughs in Six Days
- 3-Day Discover Orlando Itinerary
- Five Days in the Wild Outer Banks of North Carolina
- Two Days in Philadelphia
- Pittsburgh: Three Days Off the Beaten Path
- Day Trip from New York City: Heights of the Hudson Valley (Bridges and Ridges)

- RVA Haunts, History, and Hospitality: Three Days in Richmond, Virginia
- Savannah 3-Day Highlights Itinerary
- Three Days in the Sunshine City of St. Petersburg, Florida
- Washington, DC in 4 Days
- Washington, DC: 3 Days Like a Local

Central US

- A Laid-Back Long Weekend in Austin, TX
- 3-Day Chicago Highlights Itinerary
- 6-Hour "Layover" Chicago
- Chicago Food, Art and Funky Neighborhoods in 3 Days
- Famous Art & Outstanding Restaurants in Chicago 1-Day Itinerary
- Family Weekend in Columbus, OH
- Ohio State Game Day Weekend
- Corpus Christi: The Insider Guide for a 4-Day Tour
- The Best of Kansas City: 3-Day Itinerary
- La Grange, Kentucky: A 3-Day Tour Itinerary
- Louisville: Three Days in Derby City
- New Orleans 3-Day Itinerary
- Paris Foodie Classics: 1 Day of French Food
- Wichita From Cowtown to Air Capital in 2 Days

West Coast

- Orange County 3-Day Budget Itinerary
- Cruisin' Asbury like a Local in 1 Day
- A Day on Bainbridge Island
- Beverly Hills, Los Angeles - 1-Day Tour
- Beer Lovers 3-Day Guide To Northern California
- The Best of Boulder, CO: A Three-Day Guide
- Lesser-known Oahu in 4 Days on a Budget
- Local's Guide to Oahu - 3-Day Tour Itinerary
- Summer in Jackson Hole: Local Tips for the Perfect Three to Five Day Adventure
- Tackling 10 Must-Dos on the Big Island in 3 Days
- Las Vegas - Gaming Destination Diversions - Ultimate 3-Day Itinerary
- Las Vegas on a Budget - 3-Day Itinerary
- 2-Day Los Angeles Vegan and Vegetarian Foodie Itinerary
- Downtown Los Angeles 1-Day Walking Tour
- Hollywood, Los Angeles - 1-Day Walking Tour
- Los Angeles 4-Day Itinerary (partly using Red Tour Bus)
- Los Angeles Highlights 3-Day Itinerary
- Los Angeles On A Budget - 4-Day Tour Itinerary

- Sunset Strip, Los Angeles - 1-Day Walking Tour
- An Active 2-3 Days In Moab, Utah
- Beyond the Vine: 2-Day Napa Tour
- Wine, Food, and Fun: 3 Days in Napa Valley
- Palm Springs, Joshua Tree & Salton Sea: A 3-Day Itinerary
- Portland Bike and Bite: A 2-Day Itinerary
- Three Days Livin' as a True and Local Portlander
- Weekend Tour of Portland's Craft Breweries, Wineries, & Distilleries
- Best of the Best: Three-Day San Diego Itinerary
- San Francisco 2-Day Highlights Itinerary
- San Francisco Foodie Weekend Itinerary
- The Tech Lover's 48-Hour Travel Guide to Silicon Valley & San Francisco
- Alaska Starts Here - 3 Days in Seward
- Three Days in Central California's Wine Country
- Tucson: 3 Days at the Intersection of Mexico, Native America & the Old West

Oceania

- The Blue Mountains: A weekend of nature, culture and history.
- A Weekend Snapshot of Melbourne
- An Afternoon & Evening in Melbourne's Best Hidden Bars
- Laneway Melbourne: A One-Day Walking Tour
- Magic of Melbourne 3-Day Tour
- Two Wheels and Pair of Cozzies: the Best of Newcastle in 3 Days
- Best of Perth's Most Beautiful Sights in 3 Days
- A Weekend Snapshot of Sydney
- Sydney, Australia - 3-Day **Best Of** Itinerary
- Enjoy the Rebuild - Christchurch 2-Day Tour
- The Best of Wellington: 3-Day Itinerary

South America

- An Insider's Guide to the Best of Buenos Aires in 3 Days
- Buenos Aires Best Kept Secrets: 2-Day Itinerary
- Sights & Sounds of São Paulo - 3-Day Itinerary
- Cuenca, Ecuador - A 3-Day Discovery Tour
- A 1-Day Foodie's Dream Tour of Arequipa
- Arequipa - A 2-Day Itinerary for First-Time Visitors
- Cusco and the Sacred Valley - a five-day itinerary for a first-time visitor
- Little Known Lima 3-Day Tour

Southeast Asia

- Between the Skyscrapers - Hong Kong 3-Day Discovery Tour
- Art and Culture in Ubud, Bali – 1-Day Highlights
- Go with the Sun to Borobudur & Prambanan in 1 Day
- A 3-Day Thrilla in Manila then Flee to the Sea
- Manila on a Budget: 2-Day Itinerary
- A First Timer's Guide to 3 Days in the City that Barely Sleeps - Singapore
- Family Friendly Singapore - 3 Days in the Lion City
- Singapore: 3 Fun-Filled Days on this Tiny Island
- The Affordable Side of Singapore: A 4-Day Itinerary
- The Two Worlds of Kaohsiung in 5 Days
- 72 Hours in Taipei: The All-rounder
- Girls' Weekend in Bangkok: Shop, Spa, Savour, Swoon
- The Ins and Outs of Bangkok: A 3-Day Guide
- Saigon 3-Day Beyond the Guidebook Itinerary

Unanchor is a global family for travellers to experience the world with the heart of a local.

UNANCHOR

Made in the USA
Coppell, TX
18 January 2020